DISCOVER LANDSCAPES
Yorkshire Coast & North York Moors

JOHN POTTER

MYRIAD BOOKS

The Yorkshire Coast

THE YORKSHIRE COAST stretches from the county border at Staithes, just a few kilometres south of the river Tees in Cleveland, to Spurn Point, a long sandy promontory located on the south-eastern tip of the Holderness plain, on the northern bank of the Humber estuary. The North Yorkshire Heritage Coast forms the eastern boundary of the North York Moors National Park. This beautiful and varied landscape is unique with high rugged cliffs, traditional fishing villages, small river inlets and wide sandy bays. The long-distance footpath, the Cleveland Way, hugs the coast from the old smuggling village of Saltburn and finishes south of Scarborough at Filey, passing through some of Britain's most beautiful countryside. The larger fishing towns of Whitby, Scarborough, Bridlington and Filey are steeped in history and charm.

Staithes *right*

Staithes, known colloquially as "Steers", meaning "landing place", has a very dramatic setting on this rugged stretch of coast north of Whitby. Many of the white painted cottages are haphazardly perched on any available space and the place oozes charm and history. The sheltered harbour is reached from the cobbled main street, at the bottom of the steep hill that winds down from the busy A174 Whitby to Loftus road. Visitors are wise to leave their cars in the car park at the top of the hill and stroll at a leisurely pace down into this unspoilt fishing village.

Port Mulgrave *below*

Port Mulgrave is a tiny seaside hamlet between Hinderwell and Staithes. It was formed in the 1850s when ironstone was mined locally. The harbour pier was specially constructed at the time, but is now falling into disrepair as the North Sea takes its relentless toll. The well-marked path down through Rosedale Cliffs to the harbour is easily found at the end of the minor dead-end road from Hinderwell, but it can be very slippery after rain and visitors should be careful. There are splendid sea views to be had along the Cleveland Way between Staithes and Runswick Bay, particularly at low tide.

Runswick's cobles

Just above Runswick Bay's long
sandy beach the boat park with its
many cobles (small wooden fishing
boats) is a honeypot for artists
and photographers. The village has
a tiny Methodist chapel, an
Institute – a local meeting place
which was opened in 1870 – an
old lifeboat house and a former
coastguard house with a thatched
roof. Runswick has suffered many
times from the ravages of the
North Sea and in 1682 a landslide
destroyed the entire village with
the exception of one cottage.

Surfers' paradise

Sandsend is a pretty little fishing
village at the foot of Lythe Bank
where the sandy beach that begins
at Whitby, two miles to the south,
comes to an abrupt end. There are
many picturesque stone cottages
set against a backdrop of cliffs and
beside two meandering streams
which flow out onto the long
sandy beach. Sandsend has some
of the best surf on this coast and
a reputation as a surfers' paradise.

Whitby

Often referred to as Captain Cook's Country, the seaside town of Whitby and the surrounding countryside, from where the young James Cook drew inspiration and learned the seafarer's trade, is steeped in maritime history. Cook was born in Marton, a small village just south of Middlesbrough. His first job was in Staithes, where he assisted the merchant William Sanderson. In 1746 he took up residence in John Walker's house, an elegant 17th-century harbourside house in Grape Lane, where he served his apprenticeship and learned about navigation and seamanship. The house is now a museum which has recently been extended to include a special exhibition entitled *Curiosities from the Endeavour*, a neglected collection not seen for 200 years.

Whitby's skyline is dominated by the ruins of St Hilda's Abbey, high up on East Cliff. Just nearby, the parish church of St Mary is one of the finest Anglo-Saxon churches in the north of England. Below the church 199 steps lead down into quaint, winding narrow streets, lined with galleries, cafés, craft shops and tea rooms.

Whitby attractions

Whitby offers a host of things to do throughout the year. There are two "heritage" railways, the Esk Valley Railway Partnership and the North York Moors Railway which are both very popular, particularly with families. The author Bram Stoker (1847-1912) set much of his classic Victorian novel *Dracula* in and around the town and today visitors with a taste for the gothic can retrace the steps of the "undead" by taking the Dracula Trail Tour. The photographer Frank Meadow Sutcliffe (1853-1941) is Whitby's most famous artist. He immortalised the town and the life of its fishing community in scores of beautiful, sepia-tinted photographs many of which can be seen at the Sutcliffe Gallery.

Saltwick Bay

Access to Saltwick Bay is via a steep winding path that leads down to its soft sandy centre. On either side of this beach are vast rock platforms which are only revealed as the tide recedes. Saltwick Nab, a low rocky outcrop at the southern end of the bay, lies one mile south-east of Whitby. Close to the Nab there is the eerie outcrop known as Black Nab and at the foot of the cliff are old mineworkings and remnants of ancient breakwaters. The area is noted for fossils and the steep cliffs are constantly being eroded by the sea and the weather systems that sweep in from the North Sea.

The place has a real sense of atmosphere, particularly at first light. Many boats have come to grief on the rocks here, the most famous being the HMHS *Rohilla*, a hospital ship of 7,409 tons which belonged to the British India Steam Navigation Company. The ship smashed into a reef near Saltwick Nab on October 29 1914; of the 229 people on board, 62 crew and 28 passengers perished.

Robin Hood's Bay

The picturesque, characterful and fascinating fishing village of Robin Hood's Bay is just waiting to be explored. Its steep winding streets and cobbled ginnels (narrow alleyways between houses) are lined with old houses and cottages, many with red pantiled roofs, and everywhere there is the sound of the gulls which nest on the rooftops and chimney-stacks. Legend has it that Robin Hood once repelled Danish invaders here; during the 18th century, goods were smuggled ashore by means of secret tunnels below the houses.

Ravenscar

Ravenscar is one of the wildest and most exposed places in Yorkshire, being 183m (600ft) above sea level. The winds that blow across the North Sea sweep down from the Arctic Ocean, so it's no surprise that the once planned town was not developed. Today the 18th-century Raven Hall at the top of the cliff is a hotel and, in fact, is situated on the site of a Roman signal point. The headland is now owned by the National Trust. There are fabulous views of the sweeping Robin Hood's Bay from the coastal clifftop path, above.

The long-distance footpath, the Cleveland Way, leads north to Robin Hood's Bay and south to Ravenscar, offering ramblers and holidaymakers an abundance of spectacular views of the sea along this section, and ornithologists are often afforded close sightings of a large variety of seabirds.

Cromer Point *(above)* and Scarborough *(right)*

Cromer Point can be reached along Field Lane just east of the village of Burniston, which is 2 miles (3.22km) north of Scalby Mills and Scarborough North Bay. Tremendous views of the distant castle at Scarborough can be enjoyed here, particularly at first light; the photograph (right) is of sunrise at North Bay, Scarborough. A dismantled railway track runs parallel to the Cleveland Way along this section of the coastline and provides ramblers with an alternative path to explore.

Cromer Point is very popular with surfers, as are the coastal resorts of Runswick Bay, Sandsend Bay, Scarborough, Cayton Bay, Filey and Withernsea. Cromer Point is also an excellent spot for birdwatching and many rare species have been sighted there.

Scarborough

The ruined Norman castle and its headland dominate Scarborough's skyline. The headland stands 150ft (46m) above the harbour and, as can be seen in the photograph (below right), on a clear day a fantastic view can be enjoyed from Oliver's Mount. Right, the Spa Complex with its superb parks, gardens, theatres and conference hall sits majestically beside the principal bathing beach.

Although the harbour is now chiefly used by leisure cruisers and yachts, fish is still landed here. Scarborough became a major fishing port after Henry II built the castle in the 1170s; this led to the development of the famous Scarborough Fair, a six-week trading festival, which attracted merchants from all over Europe. The lighthouse (above), built in 1806, stands at the end of St Vincent's Pier.

Filey

Filey is an elegant and unspoilt English seaside town. Charlotte Brontë once stayed at Cliff House, now known as the Brontë Café, and other famous visitors include the composer Frederic Delius and the Mountbatten family. The five-mile sandy beach is protected from the north by the magnificent Filey Brigg. One notable feature of the town is the magnificent row of proud Victorian houses called the Crescent. Filey has many attractions including the cobbles, where small fishing boats rest at jaunty angles outside the popular beachside café. There is a week-long Edwardian festival every year in June, when strawberry teas are served by ladies in period costume. Brass bands, barrel organs and the traditional Punch and Judy show provide fun for all ages.

Bempton Cliffs

At 400ft (122m) Bempton has some of the highest cliffs on the east coast and is famous as a seabird nature reserve, featuring the only gannet colony in mainland Britain. A survey carried out by the RSPB revealed that nesting gannets had reached an all time high in 2005. In 1969 there were just 21 gannets' nests compared to 3,940 in 2005. Sadly, though, kittiwakes had their worst season in almost 20 years. Puffins (left), are a joy to watch. Their waddling walk and brightly-coloured clown-like faces make them a very endearing sight. Gannets can be seen at Bempton between January and November and are most active between April and August when they are breeding. The Bempton Cliffs nature reserve is open at all times, and the RSPB visitor centre is open daily throughout the year.

Flamborough

The coastline at Flamborough is magnificent: Thornwick Bay (above) is just one of the many sheltered shingle coves fronting the sea, and many have sea caves and dramatic stacks. The cliffs and coves teem with seabirds.

There are two schools of thought as to the origins of the place name. In the Domesday book this part of the coastline is called "Flaneberg", from the Saxon *flaen* meaning dart – a possible reference to the shape of the headland. Alternatively, the name could have developed from "the place of the flame".

Flamborough Head is famous for its lighthouse. The first was built in 1669 by Sir John Clayton, but was never kindled. The present lighthouse cost £8,000 and opened in 1806.

Bridlington *below*

Bridlington has all the essential ingredients for the perfect holiday resort. There are two glorious long sandy beaches, miles of elegant promenades, a very pretty and bustling harbour, as well as arcades, shops, amusements, restaurants and cafés. Flamborough Head and the lighthouse are clearly visible from the north pier and beach. In recent years the large fleet of trawlers has diminished and now the harbour buzzes with the sound of yachts, private fishing boats, pleasure craft and the very popular *Yorkshire Belle*. There is a lifeboat housed at Bridlington and it is launched onto a slipway from premises near the Spa Theatre. From there it is towed by tractor onto the beach.

Spurn Point

Spurn Point, situated on the north bank of the entrance to the river Humber, is a beautiful and unique place. The three-mile long finger of land that snakes out into the Humber estuary is constantly being reshaped by coastal erosion. Sea currents in this area are extremely strong and occasionally seals and porpoises can be seen here.

Spurn Point is a very important location for shipping in the area as it is the home of the Humber lighthouse, Humber pilots and the VTS (Vessel Traffic Services). Spurn Bird Observatory was opened to visitors in 1946.

Hornsea

Hornsea is a small seaside resort situated 16 miles (26km) north of Hull and 14 miles (22km) south of Bridlington. The town centre is a conservation area and some of the houses date back to the 15th century. The town is well known for the famous Hornsea Pottery which was first set up in 1949 by Desmond and Colin Rawson. In the late 1960s demand was so great that in 1970 another factory was established in Lancaster. Sadly though in 2000 the factory closed. There is also a folk museum which was established in 1978, and is housed in an 18th-century farmhouse.

Perhaps Hornsea's best known attraction is its Mere. Surprisingly the Mere is the largest freshwater lake in Yorkshire. It covers 467 acres (189ha), compared to Semerwater in the Yorkshire Dales which covers 80 acres (32.5ha). Formed by glacial deposits at the end of the last ice age it is one of many water-filled hollows, a reminder that the area once resembled the Norfolk Broads.

The Deep and the Humber Bridge

The gleaming glass and aluminium marine life centre called The Deep (left) opened in 2002. Designed by architect Sir Terry Farrell it stands at the confluence of the rivers Hull and Humber and is part of the vision of regeneration for the city of Hull. It was conceived to entertain and educate its visitors about the world's oceans and is an extremely popular visitor attraction, as well as a spectacular landmark.

The Humber Bridge (below) was designed and built to cross the last major estuary without a bridge in Britain. The north tower of this beautiful suspension bridge is sited on the high-water line and the south tower founded in shallow water 1,650ft (500m) from the shore. It is an amazing example of engineering and was developed from a design originally used for the Severn Bridge. The Humber Bridge was built to serve the communities of both north Lincolnshire and Humberside. Industry and local businesses in towns such as Immingham and Grimsby have benefited from a link to the major port of Hull and motorway connections to Manchester, Leeds and Liverpool.

North York Moors East

FROM THE PICTURESQUE and peaceful Esk Valley in the north of this region, to the vast forests of Cropton, Wykeham, Dalby and Langdale in the south, the landscape of the eastern part of the North York Moors is unique, often diverse, and extremely beautiful. The region is mostly managed for grouse and the heather is regenerated regularly by rotational burning during the winter months. There is extensive sheep grazing across the region and most flocks are reared naturally on farms along the edge of the moor in steep-sided, flat-bottomed green and fertile dales. The moorland vegetation supports large breeding populations of wading birds such as curlew, golden plover and lapwing. Also to be found on the moors are peregrine as well as merlin. A rarely seen bird, the merlin was once the hunting bird of noblewomen in the middle ages.

Scaling Dam Reservoir

The peaceful and beautiful Scaling Dam Reservoir lies just off the A171 between Guisborough and Whitby. It is the home of Scaling Dam Sailing Club which first opened in 1971. Since then it has been a thriving sailing club, offering the ideal place for families to learn to sail in safety. A wide variety of sports take place on the reservoir including general cruising, competitive races, windsurfing and fishing. Scaling is set amidst beautiful wild heather moorland, and it is a very important location for wildfowl. Part of the reservoir is protected as a nature reserve. There are good parking facilities at both ends of the reservoir, and in the summer a tea van is usually parked throughout the day at the eastern car park. The photograph (right) was taken late on a May evening just before sunset, from the eastern side of the reservoir.

Hutton-le-Hole (centre) and Glaisdale (above)

The picturesque village of Hutton-le-Hole is the home of the Ryedale Folk Museum, a "hands-on" museum with a collection of lovingly restored farm buildings where visitors can get a glimpse of the lives of ordinary people from the past to the present day.

Nestling in the Esk Valley, the village of Glaisdale is a past winner of "Village of the Year" for the North of England. The valley around Glaisdale is a majestic sight when viewed in winter from high up on the fellside (above). The area once had an abundance of iron ore and in the mid-19th century three blast furnaces were built there. Over time these became uneconomical and could not compete with the expanding steelworks.

There are two bridges over the beck in the valley bottom. One is constructed chiefly from metal and the other, called the Beggar's Bridge, is an attractive stone-built, high-arched packhorse bridge built by Thomas Ferries in 1619. He pledged to build the bridge when, during a flood, he was not able to visit his beloved Agnes, daughter of a local landowner.

Grosmont

The hillside village of Grosmont is the northern terminus for the North York Moors Railway. The village owes its existence to the railway; during the 1830s, when the railway was under construction, a rich iron deposit was discovered during tunnel building. A community soon developed around the railhead with brickworks, limekilns and blast furnaces. By 1870 the population of Grosmont had mushroomed to over 1,500 people. By the end of the 19th century the ironworks had disappeared but the village still relied entirely on the railway. It was not until 1951 that cash was raised by the villagers to build a road that linked them to the outside world.

Grosmont Station (right) has now been beautifully restored to the British Railways style of the 1960s.

Goathland

The village of Goathland can be traced back to Viking times. A custom that remains to this day is that the owners of the black-faced sheep that wander freely around the village hold common right, just as their predecessors did before them. Mallyan Spout waterfall can be reached from the footpath beside the Mallyan Hotel which leads down into West Beck gorge. The parish church of St Mary's (above) is seen here on a crisp, clear winter's day.

Beck Hole

Beck Hole is one of Yorkshire's most well-known and best-loved villages. Close by is the beautiful Mallyan Spout waterfall (left). Hidden away in a narrow wooded valley between Goathland and Grosmont, this tiny hamlet is renowned for its inn by the stone bridge and the many delightful walks that can be taken when exploring the area. In the early days of steam, on some of the steepest inclines, railway carriages were drawn by either one or two horses. Such was the severity of the slope that one particular stretch of line between Beck Hole and Goathland used a stationary engine. The Beck Hole rope winch remained in use until a fatal accident in 1864 when the rope snapped! In 1965, when many rural railway lines were closed as part of the Beeching Plan, the Pickering to Whitby line was axed after 130 years of service. It is now run by the Yorkshire Moors Preservation Society.

Littlebeck

The tiny hamlet of Littlebeck which derives its name from Little Beck, a tributary of the River Esk, lies hidden away in a very deep secluded valley on the edge of Littlebeck Wood. The roads surrounding the village have names such as Goathland Banks, Lousy Hill and Blue Bank, all of which convey the steeply-sided nature of the approach. Reaching the village is quite tricky as the roads are very narrow and caution is recommended. At the bottom of the valley there is a tiny chapel and a ford across Little Beck. A house in the village was once a school with only 13 pupils. A very pleasant woodland walk through Little Beck Wood towards the head of the valley and May Beck Wood leads to the long abandoned Midge Hall and Falling Foss Waterfall (above). The waterfall is located in a 30ft-deep gorge and access to the base of the falls should not be attempted.

Rosedale

Rosedale is a long extended valley located in the heart of the North York Moors. It stretches out in a south-easterly direction from Westerdale Moor and Danby High Moor towards Hartoft End and Cropton Forest. The river Seven flows throughout its length gathering water from the numerous moorland springs and streams. The railbed of the disused Rosedale Mineral Railway is clearly visible around the perimeter of the dale and stunning views of the valley can be enjoyed from many of the moorland paths and in particular from Chimney Bank Top. The photograph (above), looking down the valley, was taken after heavy snow, from the road near the Lion Inn on Blakey Ridge.

Rosedale Abbey

Although this delightful village is called Rosedale Abbey it has never had an abbey, but instead it was the site of a small Cistercian nunnery. Today the village is very popular with visitors and has many attractions including a tea shop, a wild flower and herb nursery, and a nine-hole golf course. The village benefits from a national park information centre, which makes an ideal starting point for exploring the village and the local moors. A short walk north of the village takes you to the slopes of North Dale from where there is a breathtaking panoramic view over Rosedale and the surrounding countryside.

The Rosedale Show (left) takes place every August and is an event the whole community looks forward to each year. The Church of St Lawrence (right) is at the heart of the village.

Hole of Horcum

This unusual feature is a huge natural amphitheatre hollowed out of the heather-clad moor situated beside the A169 Pickering to Whitby road. Legend has it that "The Devil's Punchbowl", as it is known locally, was made by a giant named Wade who scooped out the rocks and earth, tossing them two miles east to Blakey Topping.

A very popular circular walk from the roadside car park goes down through the centre of the basin and on to take in the lovely villages of Lockton and Levisham, the latter of which has an excellent inn. The walk passes by this derelict farm cottage (above) which is situated at Low Horcum. It can be quite a strenuous hike, so it is reassuring to know that there is often a mobile tea van in the car park during the summer months.

Hackness

From earliest times, visitors have been captivated by the timeless charm of this quiet and beautiful village. Hackness was first mentioned in the *Ecclesiastical History of the English People* written by the Venerable Bede in the early eighth century. Bede described how Saint Hilda, abbess of Whitby and an active figure in the early English church, founded a nunnery in Hackness in 680AD, the year of her death. St Peter's Church (below), houses a priceless Anglo-Saxon cross. When it was discovered in the 1830s it was being used as a gatepost! The cross is one of the finest examples of Anglo-Saxon Northumbrian sculpture.

Hackness is ideally suited for touring the area since it lies only five miles from the coast and the seaside resorts of Whitby and Sandsend. The Dalby Forest Drive is only a few minutes from the village by car, and close by Raincliffe Woods, Throxemby Mere and the river Derwent provide a wide variety of enticing walks for ramblers.

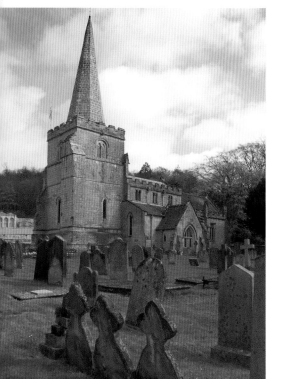

Lastingham

The village of Lastingham is a peaceful haven nestling comfortably amidst glorious scenery on the southern edge of the North York Moors and is the ideal place to stroll and relax. The area around Lastingham has much to offer with attractions such as Eden Camp Modern History Museum near Malton, the Flamingo Land theme park, Hutton Le Hole Folk Museum and many castles, stately homes, abbeys and churches.

The village is perhaps best known for the magnificent Crypt Church of St Mary, with its unique ancient crypt, which was built around 1078 as a shrine to St Chad and St Cedd who founded a Celtic monastery on this site around 645AD. The crypt is thought to be the only one in England to have an apse (rounded end) together with a chancel, nave and side aisles. There are beautiful 14th-century stained-glass windows in the north aisle.

The farmer's dog (below) is often seen patrolling the village, and can be relied upon to bark and make a fuss of walkers as they set off up the hill. Its bark is most definitely worse than its bite!

Levisham

The picturesque village of Levisham is located in the heart of the North York Moors national park and is an attractive stop on the North York Moors Railway. The small church of St John the Baptist lies at the top of the village where the road and a footpath, which meanders across woods and fields, leads to the railway station in the bottom of the valley. Birdwatchers often see hawks, woodpeckers, nuthatches, wagtails and kingfishers here. Newton Dale Hall is a walker's request stop on the steam train and a starting point for many lovely walks. The station has been used as the location for a range of television programmes including *All Creatures Great and Small*.

Troutsdale

Situated north of Stainton on the Pickering to Scarborough road, Troutsdale (below) and Rosekirk Dale Fens are designated Sites of Special Scientific Interest. These two areas of fenland are rich in spring and flush fen which grows well in the local area due to energy-rich springs which flow from the Corallian limestone underground. Fen sytems like these are rare nationally and are only found in areas of Oxfordshire, Norfolk, Anglesey and North Yorkshire. Rushes, sedges, valerian, meadowsweet, meadowthistle and several species of orchid all flourish here. These fen beds and the surrounding moorland make Troutsdale a haven of peace and seclusion.

Thornton Le Dale

Thornton Le Dale lies just east of Pickering on the A170 Scarborough road. In the centre of the town is a small green, a market cross and stocks. The village has gift shops, tea rooms, and a large tench pond near the main car park; alongside the roads to Malton and Scarborough a shimmering stream tumbles over a bed of cobbles. The cottage (below) is possibly one of the most photographed in North Yorkshire.

Pickering

The busy and elegant market town of Pickering (right) is located on the southern edge of the North York Moors where the A170 Thirsk to Scarborough road crosses the A169 Malton to Whitby road. It was originally a Celtic town dating from the 3rd century BC, and has a motte-and-bailey castle with Norman remnants. In the centre of the town is Beck Isle Museum of Rural Life, housed in a Grade 2 listed Regency

mansion. The museum has 27 galleries and visitors are transported back through time as they pass through a variety of recreated settings including a cobblers' shop, blacksmiths, chemists' shop, dairy and village store. Of particular interest is the gallery which features the work of local photographer Sydney Smith who captured the atmosphere of rural life in and around Pickering in the late 19th and early 20th centuries. He is thought of as a successor to Frank Meadow Sutcliffe of Whitby. The Church of St Peter & St Paul has some rare medieval paintings uncovered in the middle of the 19th century.

Pickering Steam

A major annual attraction is the Pickering Traction Engine Rally. Held on the showground, it is a four-day event with literally hundreds of lovingly restored and spectacular steam engines, vintage tractors, miniature steam engines, vintage and classic cars, fairground organs, military vehicles and motorcycles. The extravaganza of steam and fun appeals to people of every age, as can be seen in the photograph (right). Billed as the north's biggest steam event, the show has two vast arenas which stage several live shows. There are also army displays, Punch and Judy shows, a road run to Pickering and a fireworks display.

North York Moors West

THE NORTH YORK MOORS is a place where it is possible to unwind and enjoy some of the finest landscapes in Britain. Considerably drier than the Pennine moors to the west, the windswept purple heather-clad moors, lush green dales and vast expanses of woodland are characteristic of this unique area.

In the west the national park is bounded by the Hambleton and the Cleveland Hills. James Herriot, the author, once described the breathtaking view from Sutton Bank as the finest in England. Walk just a few miles along the escarpment from the national park visitor centre at the top of Sutton Bank and it is very easy to see just what he meant. Over eight centuries ago the abbot St Aelred, in describing the magnificent Rievaulx Abbey, just north of Helmsley, said "Everywhere peace, everywhere serenity, and a marvellous freedom from the tumult of the world." It is without doubt these very same experiences that compel visitors to return again and again to this captivating region.

Castleton

Situated in the upper Esk Valley, the linear village of Castleton sits proudly on a high ridge, where the lush green secluded valleys of Westerdale and Danby Dale come together on the northern fringe of the North York Moors. The village has a Quaker graveyard with gravestones dated from 1815 to 1944. A quick survey reveals that the majority of names on the stones have the surname of Puckrin. Remains of the old castle, built by Robert De Brus, are now part of a large house. Most of the castle was dismantled in 1216, and around 1240 some of the stones were used to restore Danby Church. The distant view of the village in winter (above), was taken from Castleton Rigg looking north-east towards Danby Park Wood and Haw Rigg.

Westerdale

The monument named Young Ralph Cross (right) stands proud, next to the symbol marking the geological centre of the North York Moors; in 1974 it was adopted as the emblem of the national park. The cross was erected in the 18th century where an earlier named cross, Crux Radulph, once stood. Records of the cross go as far back as 1200 and in 1550 it was constructed of wood. It is said that the present cross was erected in memory of a destitute traveller who died from exhaustion. A Danby farmer called Ralph discovered him and later decided to erect a cross where he found the body.

There is clear evidence on the moor above Dale View in Westerdale that the area has been inhabited since at least the Bronze Age. At Cairnfield around one hundred individual cairns and traces of metal workings have been discovered including an axe-hammer and other prehistoric remains.

Blakey Ridge

The views from Blakey Ridge across both Rosedale to the east and Farndale to the west are quite simply breathtaking, particularly after heavy snow. This early morning photograph (above) taken from the side of the Hutton-le-Hole to Castleton road, just north of the Lion Inn, reveals the head of Rosedale valley in all its splendour. The distant ridge, Nab Scar, just below Sturdy Bank, is where the dismantled railway bed runs around the east rim of Rosedale.

The world-famous coast-to-coast trail from St Bees in Cumbria to Robin Hood's Bay, devised by Alfred Wainwright, takes in Blakey Ridge. The 24 mile (38km) stretch from Clay Bank over Blakey Ridge, and then on to Grosmont, goes through remote moorland.

Another long-distance trail, the Lyke Wake Walk, a 41 mile (67km) route passes near the Lion Inn, a tourist honeypot, where real ales, a cosy atmosphere and good food can always be guaranteed. Every July the music festival draws thousands of visitors to this stunning setting to enjoy the event where live bands perform.

Farndale

The tiny and picturesque hamlet of Church Houses (right) nestles between the mighty Rudland Rigg and Blakey Ridge in glorious scenery at the heart of this much-loved dale. Perhaps best known for its wild daffodils in spring, Farndale attracts up to 40,000 visitors each April. The daffodil walk follows the valley bottom (below) beside the river Dove, from Low Mill to Church Houses. Pictured in spring,

Church Houses and the distant winding minor road leading up to Blakey Ridge, were photographed from Daleside Road at the foot of Horn Ridge. A footpath leads down from Daleside Road to Church Houses where walkers can savour fabulous views of the distant Potter's Nab and High Blakey Moor.

Below right, looking toward the valley bottom in winter.

Gillamoor

The pretty village of Gillamoor (above) lies 2.5 miles (4km) north of Kirby Moorside on the minor road that links Fadmoor to Hutton Le Hole. The village is famously known for its Surprise View at the eastern end of the hamlet, beside St Aidan's Church. The view of lower Farndale from this point is memorable whatever the season.

Helmsley

This is one of the prettiest country towns in North Yorkshire. Located on the Thirsk to Scarborough road, Helmsley is a very popular destination and an ideal centre for touring the local area. The market square is surrounded by a wide variety of gift shops, pubs, restaurants and galleries and on most weekends there is a lively atmosphere. A pretty stream runs through the town at the back of the market square (below) complete with stone arch bridge.

The poet William Wordsworth stayed at the Black Swan Inn in the centre of the town when courting Mary, his future wife. Helmsley Castle is a spectacular ruin and once guarded the Rye Valley. The early 13th-century castle is surrounded by a formidable double ditch cut from solid rock. It was once known as Furstan Castle. Sir Charles Duncombe purchased the castle after it was rendered useless by Oliver Cromwell and it has subsequently been owned by the Earls of Feversham who are descended from Sir Charles. The Feversham family live in the Vanbrugh-built mansion in nearby Duncombe Park on the edge of the village.

Rievaulx Abbey

Traditionally Cistercian abbeys were built on an east-west axis, but because of the steep slope at Rievaulx a north-south alignment was adopted. Like all Cistercian houses the location was deliberately secluded from the outside world and this particular site in the depths of the narrow river Rye valley must have provided the monks and lay brethren with a haven of peace and solitude. The 13th-century church is reputed to have been one of the finest monastic churches in northern Britain and thankfully remains substantially intact. The abbey site is now owned and run by English Heritage, whereas Rievaulx Terrace and Temples (below), situated on an escarpment above the abbey, is owned by the National Trust. From this elevated position tremendous views of the abbey and valley are to be enjoyed. Recent archaeological discoveries show that the monks once ate wild strawberries and that there used to be a flourishing iron industry at the site.

Old Byland

The tiny and peaceful hamlet of Old Byland (right) is located just west of Rievaulx Abbey in the south-west corner of the North Yorks Moors. The village consists of a few stone cottages and farm buildings surrounding a small village green. The church of All Saints is steeped in history and there has been a church of one kind or another on this site since Saxon times. Following the Norman Conquest the area was ravaged by William the Conqueror's army. The Domesday Book records for 1086 state that only two settlements, Helmsley and Old Byland, survived and that there was "a priest and a wooden church" in the village.

Boltby

Nestling in a deep narrow valley just west of the Hambleton Hills and two miles north of Gormire Lake, Boltby (left) is a delightfully quiet and peaceful village. Its name derives from the Danish *boltebi* and it is mentioned in the Domesday Book. The village street is lined with attractive stone and brick cottages; in its centre is Holy Trinity Church.

The village has a population of approximately 170, and an "on demand" bus service on Mondays to the bustling market town of Thirsk. Walkers along the Cleveland Way footpath should consider taking a slight detour in order to explore this lovely hamlet in its tranquil setting. A pretty stone bridge straddles Gurtof Beck which runs under the road, and occasionally over it, after heavy rain!

Sutton Bank

Views from Sutton Bank over the Vale of York and Mowbray towards the Yorkshire Dales are deservedly considered to be some of the finest in the north of England. The Hambleton Escarpment rises abruptly to a height of around 1,000ft (300m) and you can often see for more than 30 miles (50km). Gormire Lake (above) is silhouetted by a dramatic sky stirred up by strong winds sweeping impatiently across the Vale of York. Gormire, which is semi-circular in shape, is one of only a few true lakes in Yorkshire and Gormire Rigg is a glacial feature creating a retaining bowl-shaped bank behind the lake.

Unusually, there are no streams in or out of the lake. Just beyond Roulston Scar lies the well-known landmark the White Horse of Kilburn, built by local teacher John Hodgson and his pupils in 1857.

The Cleveland Way

Whitestone Cliff (left) on the Cleveland Way footpath looking north towards the village of Boltby. The Cleveland Way starts in the market town of Helmsley and traverses the upland ridge on the edge of the North York Moors before reaching the coast at Saltburn by the Sea. It then continues along the Heritage Coast and ends at Filey – a distance of 110 miles (177km). The footpath is really two walks in one, the first a walk across high moorland while the second is a walk along one of the most outstanding sections of coastline in Britain.

First published in 2010 by Myriad Books Limited
35 Bishopsthorpe Road, London SE26 4PA

Photographs copyright © John Potter
Text copyright © John Potter

ISBN 1 84746 348 7
EAN 978 1 84746 348 7

Designed by Jerry Goldie Graphic Design

Printed in China

www.myriadbooks.com